JEDEDIAH SMITH

Mountain Man of the American West

CHARLES W.
MAYNARD

The Rosen Publishing Group's
PowerKids Press™
New York

For Caroline and Jamie, who are exploring new territory

Published in 2003 by The Rosen Publishing Group, Inc.
29 East 21st Street, New York, NY 10010

First Edition

Managing Editor: Kathy Kuhtz Campbell
Book Designer: Maria E. Melendez

Photo Credits: Cover and title page, © The Kansas State Historical Society; p. 4 © National Geographic Society; p. 7 courtesy Joselyn Art Museum, Omaha, Nebraska; p. 8 (top left) Prints and Photography Division, Library of Congress; p. 8 (bottom) © SuperStock; p. 11 © National Museum of American Art, Washington, D.C./Art Resource, New York; p. 12 courtesy of the General Research and Humanities Division, The New York Public Library, Astor, Lenox, and Tilden Foundations; p. 15 © SuperStock; p. 16 © Pat O'Hara/CORBIS, p. 17 © N. Carter/North Wind Picture Archives; p. 19 © CORBIS; p. 20 Smithsonian American Art Museum, Washington, D.C./Art Resource, New York.

Maynard, Charles W. (Charles William), 1955–
Jedediah Smith : mountain man of the American West / Charles W. Maynard.— 1st ed.
p. cm. — (Famous explorers of the American West)
Includes bibliographical references and index.
Summary: Follows the life of the nineteenth-century trapper and explorer who earned his reputation on the western frontier.
ISBN 0-8239-6287-3 (library binding)
1. Smith, Jedediah Strong, 1799–1831—Juvenile literature. 2. Pioneers—West (U.S.)—Biography—Juvenile literature. 3. Explorers—West (U.S.)—Biography—Juvenile literature. 4. Trappers—West (U.S.)—Biography—Juvenile literature. 5. Frontier and pioneer life—West (U.S.)—Juvenile literature. 6. West (U.S.)—Discovery and exploration—Juvenile literature. 7. West (U.S.)—History—To 1848—Juvenile literature. 8. West (U.S.)—Biography—Juvenile literature. [1. Smith, Jedediah Strong, 1799–1831. 2. Explorers. 3. West (U.S.)—Discovery and exploration.] I. Title. II. Series.
F592.S6514 M39 2003
978'.02'092—dc21

2001005464

Manufactured in the United States of America

CONTENTS

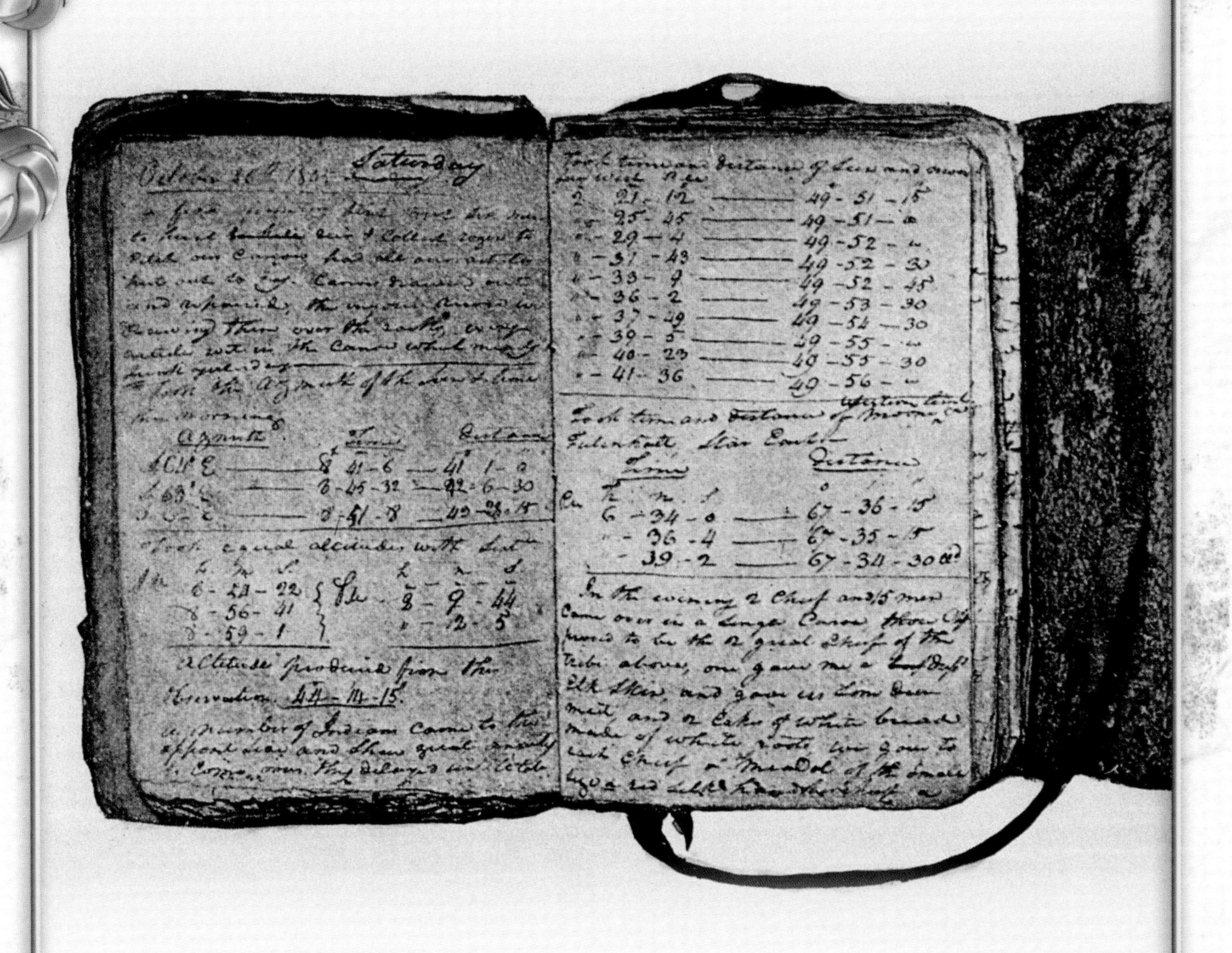

William Clark carried this elk-skin-bound journal with him during his 1804–1806 journey to the Pacific Ocean. Smith carried copies of Clark's and Meriwether Lewis's journals on all of his travels.

MOVING WEST

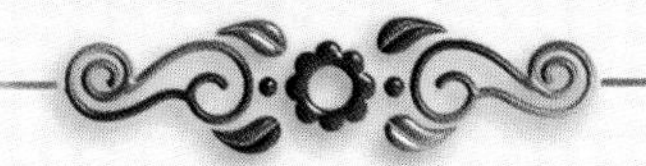

Jedediah Strong Smith was born on January 6, 1799, to Sally and Jedediah Smith. Jedediah was the sixth of fourteen children. The Smiths lived near Jericho, New York. In the early 1800s, many Americans went west to find land for farming. The Smiths moved to the shores of Lake Erie in Ohio.

A family story tells that a friend gave young Jedediah a set of books. The books were copies of Meriwether Lewis's and William Clark's **journals**. Lewis and Clark explored the **Louisiana Purchase** to find a western water route to the Pacific Ocean. Jedediah loved to read about their **explorations**.

In 1821, Jedediah left his family and traveled to St. Louis, Missouri, to find work. He answered an 1822 **advertisement** calling for "**Enterprising** Young Men," to go to the western mountains.

A MOUNTAIN MAN

Jedediah Smith became a mountain man when he joined General William Ashley and Major Andrew Henry and their company of fur trappers in 1822. People called fur trappers "mountain men," because these men went to the Rocky Mountains to trap beavers. From about 1820 to 1840, beaver fur clothing was popular in the East and in Europe. Fur companies hired trappers to hunt beavers, because beaver **pelts** were used to make hats and capes.

Mountain men set traps to catch beavers. A long pole held an iron trap in shallow water. A chain attached it to the shore. The mountain man waded in the stream to bait the trap with castor oil. This oil came from a gland near the base of a beaver's tail, and its smell attracted other beavers.

Smith, like the other trappers, looked for streams in which to hunt. He explored many unfamiliar areas in search of beavers.

Most beaver hunting was done in the cold days of late fall and early spring, when a beaver's fur was thickest. Mountain men set traps in the icy cold water at dusk and checked them at dawn.

Edward S. Curtis photographed Bear's Belly, an Arikara, around 1908. Smith's group of mountain men reached an Arikara village in May 1823. After a battle broke out, 14 men in Smith's group were killed and 9 were wounded.

George Caleb Bingham painted Fur Traders Descending the Missouri *around 1845. Smith and other fur trappers left St. Louis, Missouri, in May 1822 to begin exploring and hunting around the Missouri River.*

A SURPRISE BATTLE

In the winter of 1822–1823, 22-year-old Jedediah Smith hunted food for his fellow fur trappers. The trappers camped at a small **fort** near where the Musselshell River poured into the Missouri River. Smith walked or rode on horseback, hunting for animals for food, while many of the others paddled up the Missouri River.

After the winter Major Andrew Henry, who led the men, sent Smith down the river to meet General William Ashley. Ashley was coming up the river to bring supplies and men. Smith carried a message that told Ashley to buy horses from the Native Americans called the **Arikara**. While the men were trading for horses, a battle broke out. Smith was caught at the river amid the gunfire. As shots were fired all around, he swam to safety.

A GRIZZLY ATTACK

In September 1823, after the battle with the Arikara, Smith led a small group of about 20 trappers. They went into the Black Hills of today's South Dakota. While Smith was hunting, he was attacked by a large grizzly bear. The bear knocked him from his horse. The huge, angry bear broke several of Smith's ribs and tore off one ear and much of his scalp.

One of the other men, Jim Clyman, used a needle and thread to sew together Smith's wounds. When Clyman said he could not sew on Smith's ear, the wounded Smith asked Clyman to try. Ten days later, Smith had recovered enough to command the small group again. After the bear attack, he always wore his hair long to cover the horrible scars.

A grizzly bear attacked Smith while he was hunting in the Black Hills. Grizzlies can be 7 feet (2 m) tall and can weigh from 325 to 850 pounds (147–386 kg). George Catlin painted this grizzly around 1847.

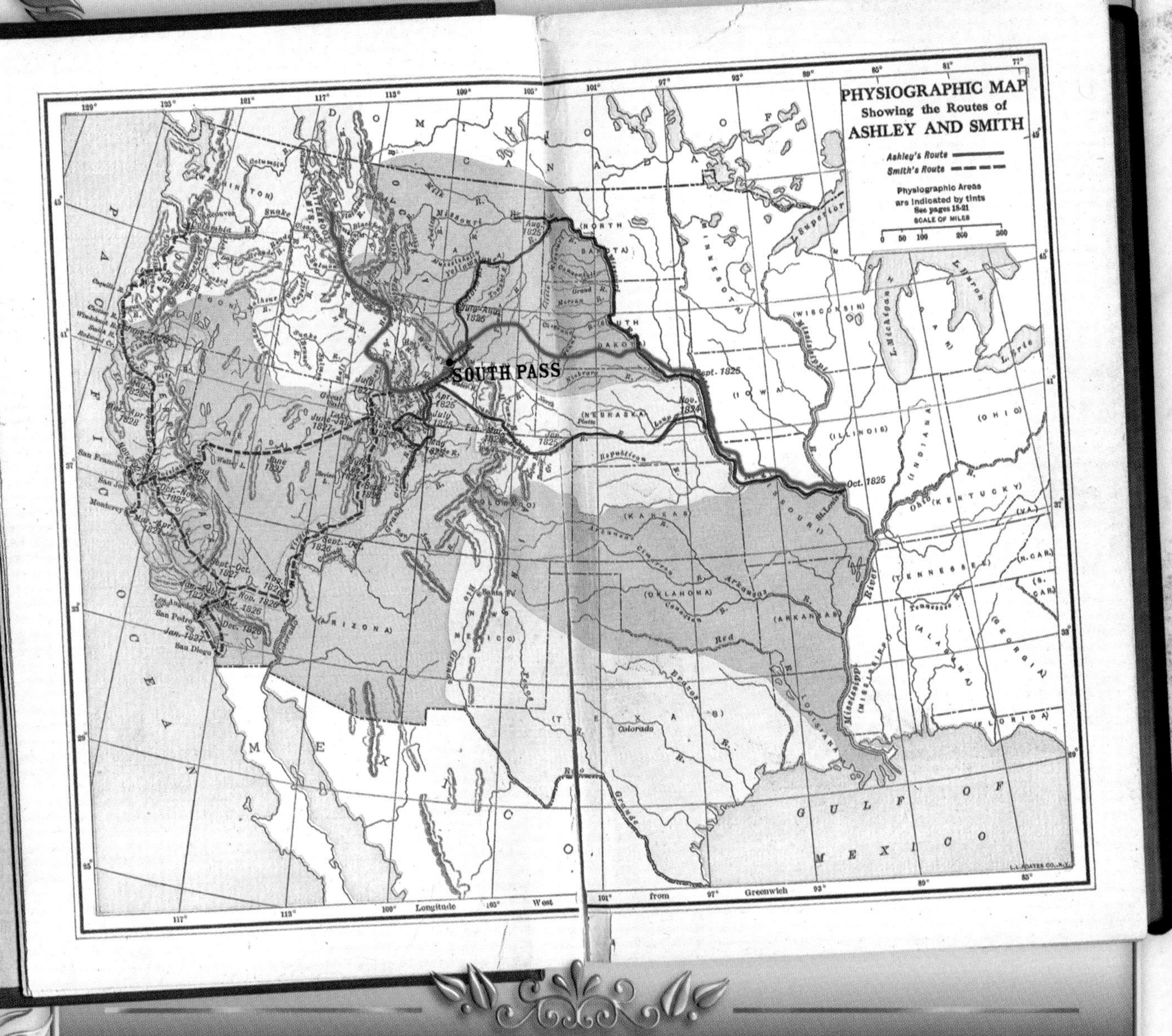

This map shows some of the routes that Smith and Ashley traveled from 1822 to 1828. The blue route shows the way Smith went when he first traveled through the South Pass. Robert Stuart had discovered South Pass in 1812, but not many people remembered his discovery. Smith told others that wagons could be driven through it.

SOUTH PASS

The winter after the grizzly attack, Smith and his men lived in a Crow village near the Wind River Mountains of today's Wyoming. The Crow were Native Americans who lived on the Great Plains and in the Rocky Mountains. In March 1824, the men decided to cross the Rocky Mountains to find more beavers. Deep snow blocked the passes through the peaks. The wind blew so hard that fires could not be lit. Food could not be cooked without fire. The men were freezing and hungry. Smith and others found their way over the Rockies through a low mountain pass. This pass, called South Pass, rose along the Sweetwater River and crossed to the Green River. Smith and his men told others that wagons could be driven over the Rockies through South Pass to Oregon or to California.

CROSSING THE DESERT

In 1826, Jedediah Smith joined two friends in forming a new fur company. Smith took 17 men to the Great Salt Lake. They explored along the Sevier and Virgin Rivers. **Paiute** living nearby shared pumpkins and squash to keep the men from starving.

Smith led the men across the **Mojave** Desert into California. This journey was the first recorded overland trip to California. In 1826, everyone who went to California traveled by sea. Smith left most of his men in California while he and two friends returned to the Great Salt Lake for supplies in the spring of 1827. There he gathered 18 men to return to California. As they crossed the Colorado River, a band of Mojave **ambushed** them, and killed 10 of Smith's men. Those who stayed alive crossed the Mojave Desert into California in only 9 ½ days.

Smith's 1826 crossing of the Mojave Desert took 15 days in terrible heat. In the 1827 return trip, Smith and his two friends buried themselves in sand during the day to cool off, and traveled at night.

Snow dusts the White Mountains in the Sierra Nevada in California. In 1827, Smith and his group of mountain men had to cross the Sierra Nevada on their way to California and Oregon.

A DISCOVERY

The remaining men followed Jedediah Smith to rejoin his men in California. These mountain men trapped beavers in the mountains of northern California and Oregon. Smith loved to explore new territory. He kept a journal and drew maps of all of his travels.

Travel was difficult. Each day Smith left the camp ahead of the group to scout a route through the forest. One day they found a 10-year-old **Willamette** boy who had been held as a slave by other Native Americans. Smith and his men made friends with the boy and called him Marion. They tried to return Marion to his people.

Fur trappers, including Native Americans, killed so many beavers for their fur that by the early 1840s, hardly any beavers were left. Even other animals, such as buffalo and fox, became scarce because they were hunted for their pelts.

AMBUSHED

On July 14, 1828, Smith and two men left their camp to go up the river to scout. This river later was named the Smith River after Jedediah Smith. While the three men were away, **Kelwatset** men ambushed and killed 15 people, including the young boy, Marion, in the camp. Only one person from the group left in the camp got away. The Kelwatset attacked because they were angry over their ill treatment by white people.

The four men who were left, including Smith, went into Oregon to Fort Vancouver on the Columbia River to be safe from more attacks.

The Hudson's Bay Company established Fort Vancouver as its chief fur-trading post in 1825. When Smith headed to the fort for safety in 1828, it was the chief supply post for furs being shipped to England.

TIMELINE

1799 On January 6, Jedediah Smith is born near Jericho, New York.

1810 The Smith family moves to Erie County, Pennsylvania.

1817 The Smith family moves to the western area of Ohio.

1821 Jedediah leaves his family and goes to Illinois.

1822 Smith joins Ashley and Henry's fur company.

1823 In May the mountain men battle with the Arikara.
In October a grizzly bear attacks Smith.

1824 In March Smith and his men go through South Pass.

1826 In July Smith and two friends form a fur-trading partnership.
In November Smith crosses the Mojave Desert into California.

1827 In June Smith crosses the Great Basin to the Great Salt Lake.
In August the Mojave attack Smith's men on the Colorado River.

1828 In July the Kelwatset attack and kill 15 people on today's Smith River in northern California.

1830 Smith returns to St. Louis.

1831 On May 27, Comanche kill Smith on the Santa Fe Trail.

A band of Comanche surrounded Jedediah Smith in May 1831. Smith was searching for water along the Santa Fe Trail.

THE FINAL RENDEZVOUS

Mountain men gathered each summer for a meeting called a **rendezvous**. Native Americans and trappers traded furs for gunpowder and supplies. They also told stories about their travels.

In the summer of 1830, Smith came to the rendezvous on the Wind River in today's central Wyoming. During his eight years in the West, he had crossed high peaks and burning sands. He and his partners sold their company and went to St. Louis. While in St. Louis, Smith wrote to his family back in Ohio to tell them he was okay. He showed his own maps to General Ashley, who later shared them with mapmakers. Smith began working on his journals so that he could publish them. Although his journals and letters were not published until 1934, his explorations were not forgotten.

SMITH'S LEGACY

Jedediah Smith had to take a business trip to Santa Fe in 1831, using the Santa Fe Trail. At this time Santa Fe was part of Mexico. His men ran out of water, so Smith rode ahead to find some. While Smith was alone, a band of **Comanche** surrounded him. He made signs of peace to them. A Comanche shot him with arrows. Smith fired his weapon back, killing a Comanche. The group then killed Smith.

Smith had accomplished many great feats. He rediscovered South Pass. He was the first to enter California from the east by crossing the Mojave Desert. He crossed the Great Basin Desert and returned east from California, proving that the deserts could be crossed safely. Many people who helped to settle the West followed the trails Smith had blazed to California and Oregon.

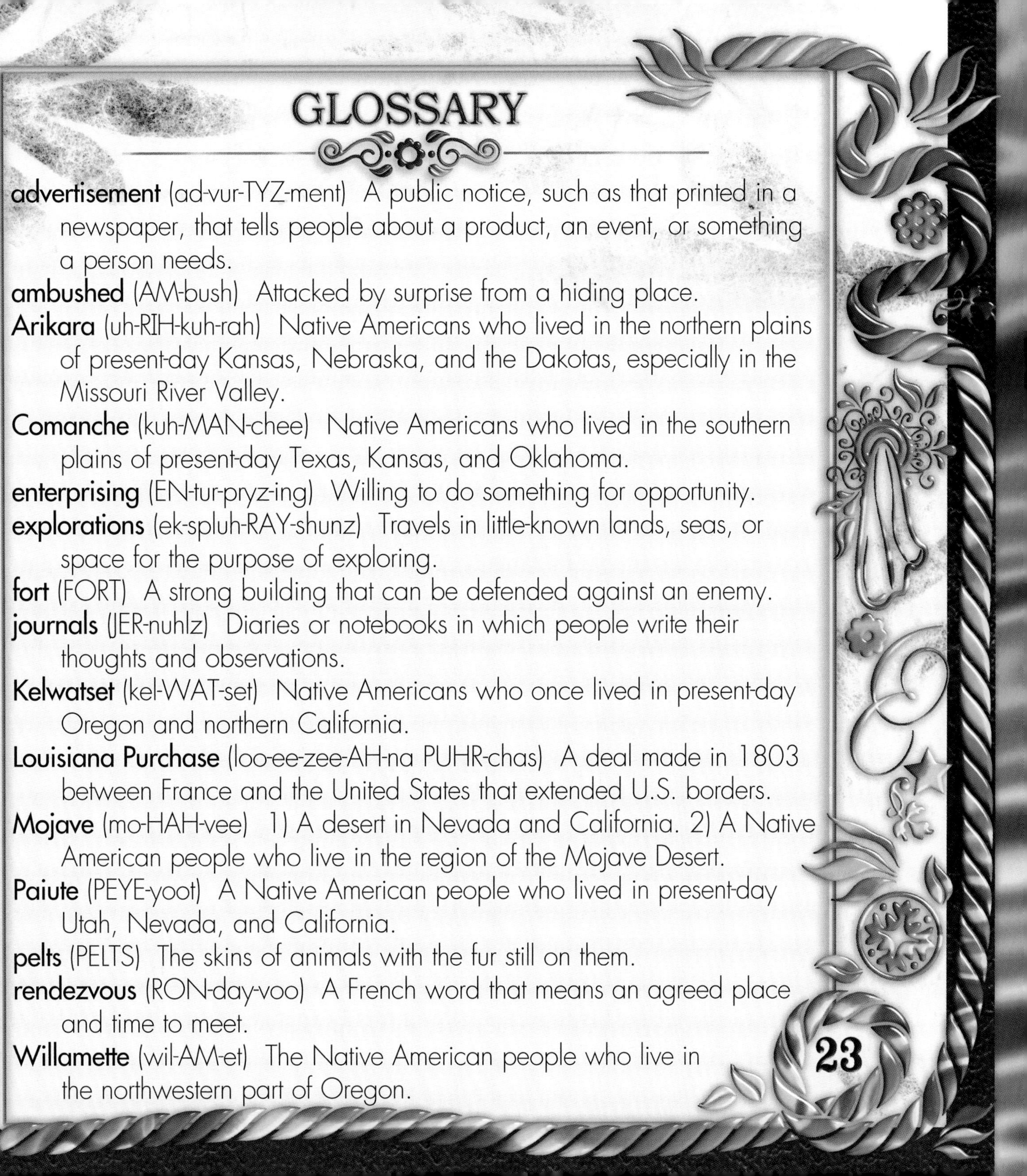

GLOSSARY

advertisement (ad-vur-TYZ-ment) A public notice, such as that printed in a newspaper, that tells people about a product, an event, or something a person needs.

ambushed (AM-bush) Attacked by surprise from a hiding place.

Arikara (uh-RIH-kuh-rah) Native Americans who lived in the northern plains of present-day Kansas, Nebraska, and the Dakotas, especially in the Missouri River Valley.

Comanche (kuh-MAN-chee) Native Americans who lived in the southern plains of present-day Texas, Kansas, and Oklahoma.

enterprising (EN-tur-pryz-ing) Willing to do something for opportunity.

explorations (ek-spluh-RAY-shunz) Travels in little-known lands, seas, or space for the purpose of exploring.

fort (FORT) A strong building that can be defended against an enemy.

journals (JER-nuhlz) Diaries or notebooks in which people write their thoughts and observations.

Kelwatset (kel-WAT-set) Native Americans who once lived in present-day Oregon and northern California.

Louisiana Purchase (loo-ee-zee-AH-na PUHR-chas) A deal made in 1803 between France and the United States that extended U.S. borders.

Mojave (mo-HAH-vee) 1) A desert in Nevada and California. 2) A Native American people who live in the region of the Mojave Desert.

Paiute (PEYE-yoot) A Native American people who lived in present-day Utah, Nevada, and California.

pelts (PELTS) The skins of animals with the fur still on them.

rendezvous (RON-day-voo) A French word that means an agreed place and time to meet.

Willamette (wil-AM-et) The Native American people who live in the northwestern part of Oregon.

INDEX

PRIMARY SOURCES

Page 4. *William Clark's journal.* This elk-skin-bound journal of Clark's 1804–1806 expedition is in the Missouri Historical Society's collection in St. Louis. **Page 7.** *Setting Traps for Beaver.* Alfred Jacob Miller painted these trappers in the Green River in the1830s. Miller was the first artist to record the life of the mountain men. The painting is in the collection of the Joselyn Art Museum, Omaha, Nebraska. **Page 12.** *Physiographic Map.* This map was first published in 1920 in *The Splendid Wayfaring: The Story of the Exploits and Adventures of Jedediah Smith and His Comrades, the Ashley-Henry Men, Discoverers and Explorers of the Great Central Route from the Missouri River to the Pacific Ocean, 1822–1831* by John G. Neihardt. The blue route showing the path Smith took to South Pass has been added to the 1920 map by PowerKids Press for the purpose of this book. Neihardt was a poet with a life-long interest in the culture of Native Americans and in the experiences of fur trappers in the West. **Page 20.** *Comanche War Party, Mounted on Wild Comanche Horses.* George Catlin painted this picture from 1834 to 1837. Today it is in the collection of the National Museum of American Art, Smithsonian Institution, Washington, D.C.

WEB SITES

To learn more about Jedediah Smith, check out these Web sites:
http://xroads.virginia.edu/~HYPER/HNS/Mtmen/jedesmith.html
www.desertusa.com/mag99/feb/papr/jsmith.html